HORSES
/HOOTSO

Jake Skeets is the author of *Eyes Bottle Dark with a Mouthful of Flowers* and winner of the National Poetry Series, Kate Tufts Discovery Award, American Book Award and Whiting Award. His writing has appeared in *Poetry Foundation*, *The New York Times Magazine* and *The Paris Review*.

Skeets is the recipient of an NEA Grant and a Mellon Projecting All Voices Fellowship. He is Diné, from the Navajo Nation, and is currently serving as the 3rd Navajo Nation Poet Laureate, 2025–2027.

'Behind these poems is a reverberation of horse songs echoing, holding tight at the borders. Grief is a primary material, here rendered into beauty, and as you listen you will hear, feel, and know that beauty is possible even when it appears impossible. An astounding book.'
– Joy Harjo

'With its gorgeously wrought poems that both eulogize and praise, *Horses* is a singularly stunning collection. Skeets is a poet singing back to the often-frightening world; how lucky we are to overhear this awestruck music.'
– Ada Limón

'There is so much to take notice of and be enriched by in Jake Skeets' mesmerizing *Horses*. His use of language is so precise and considered it makes me feel that English can be something besides what history has made of it. *Horses* is a lifeline thrown "through an open window" toward us. A stunning achievement.'
– Billy-Ray Belcourt

'Skeets' long-awaited second collection brims with disquiet and landscapes that catalog not only what beauty survives in the Anthropocene, but also what violently departs . . . His lyric lingers in my mind like the fine echo of a violin through a canyon.'
– Diana Khoi Nguyen

'Written to sing the end of the world, instead he sees a new one: one of potential, breath, language, dreaming, ritual, making, and meaning.'
– Pádraig Ó Tuama

HORSES /HOOTSO

Jake Skeets

LONDON

for the land

Contents

Just Before the Silence	xiii
Horses	1
Hootso	21
Entanglements I	51
And Still Deer Soften	81
Notes	117
A Failed Glossary	121
On the Poems	123
Acknowledgements	125

Then Space – began to toll,

As all the Heavens were a Bell,
And Being, but an Ear,
And I, and Silence, some strange Race,
Wrecked, solitary, here –

—EMILY DICKINSON

just before the silence

                        a circle of horses in a brightening storm

I carry sound

on the range the sun holds its head low

I carry wind

there is nothing but sand here

I carry morning

the door crickets and sprawls in an open field

I carry light

but just a bend of it : an echo around a face

HORSES

PART ONE   CARRIER

first, the sky pronounced on red soil—its want to be more holy
to be more whole, its promise its gesture like a rock
up a gentle slope or one long body wrapped around a map
a curved mirror

it carries time and emissions shifted through scattered grasses
over a six- to nine-month period ahum adrift aloft alone
a gallery of altitudes and at any given time a field of regard
a field of snow a field of too much light

there, a wasp a glottis a stirring of teeth
the letters we carry over the spit of high moon and morning coffee
somewhere in a canyon on the roadway a sudden river
washing away god

we become lightning sometimes and there
only then become song, carry our ache, its kick pull haul hull
become dark cattle a body of water the mouth around light
dark clouds leaping into a cold wind

PART TWO   APOCALYPSE

there has been no rain and we monster
hot afternoons in narrow hollows
metals green and sweep over memories of dew
and shorelines now rust and golden with sweat
from dry wild weeds – lake late
heads thrown back : steel beams and all

there, we trace the outline of bay horses in our legs
in the red rocks on the backs of ladybugs
our hands smell of burning coal
sauntered fox light and elk-borne winters
birds still sing and from the jaw of a pale sky
dark clouds kneel like you would a shadow

there are ways nature plants a mirror
so each hill and heat burst look the same
between the ways time has a body
in the layers of skin each a different shade or century
a rill of vowels with different faces reflect
the sun in new light every time

there, each new eternity collapsed
into mineral strata
on a canyon wall in winter drought
as in a mirror touching time
like it would our bodies
dreaming our bodies

PART THREE   MEMORIAL

I trace the outline
of horses encased
in hydrated lime
      an offering
to return bone
to loam to ground water

the horses buried
on-site to free up
the creeks and crease of their pasts
their makeup all song
and morning and mane

here, enshrined
with the memory
of a stock pond
horses buried
thigh-deep in mud
clawing for the first world
for something we left behind

PART FOUR   SENTENCE

one wide field of shrubbery and tumbleweed before it is pulled and becomes part air and flows back into a sentence   there are no ways to discuss a sentence here because sentences become one long horizon one can see all around them with no break or utter just weeds and foothills that twist themselves into a memory of winter frost or hay wire only to be crushed beneath steel-toe boots and the sentence drags their body from a sleeping horse that forgets to shake snow off itself and the sentence continues down the fence line into the mouth of a semicolon before it drags its body across the plateau or whatever this place is called the word *plateau* derived from *plat* which translates to *wide* as in *platform* as in *page* as in *white space* as in *land* as in *a mountain would have been here* but the land stretched itself out to create a platform a page so one could see how far they would have to drag themselves to get to the road because even in open spaces one can be invisible like the snow that falls here is invisible like hills that should break the horizon are invisible and black sand and white snow on the page on the platform on the plateau forgets its own bruises and lays itself flat perhaps in an attempt to *float*

PART FIVE   SOUND

what sound does a river make :
grocery store carts
a freeway a few yards east of us
geese on the roadside
room glow ribboned through fingers
of the words *angostura* or *alluvium*
and still deer soften into grasses
in ghost lakes we still hear the sound of them
the sound a mouth forms around an *h*

hymn   hue   whole

howl   whim   *wind*

PART SIX   REVERE

because even clouds can't stand this heat;
the sky is memoryless
the color of drying wool
        hung over a wire

because even in a beat-up car
I find a way to locust through
sputter through pollen and reed
consciousness and afternoon

        sun pours through
a chimney hole and I build a hogan
to fill with hay bales – only to find my mother
making bread by the stove

telling me run to the east
in the first light of final light

PART SEVEN   TIME

I am obsessed with coal mines because summer
because time milled like grain in one long day
        too hot for shadow

they speak through glass breaking in an empty room
I wake to the sound of rainwater on the windshield
        of my past

I get up to leave but suddenly it's June
no matter how tight I stretch my muscles
        at first thunder

if light were a liquid what then of night
with its teeth gnashed like a belt of stars
        withholding time

PART EIGHT   DUST DEVIL

I reach my hands
                      into blowing dust ;
and it takes something from me

      (my eyes water)   –

storms coat night algae slept into a misty field
                    a horse offers something in return :
lungs of evaporated milk ; then,

      (   )   (the hills water)

PART NINE   GENESIS

through charcoal and reef

                        a jaw held in oil and century

in its mouth

                        wet snow or rotting cedar trees

crooned from low currents

                        light condemned to spine

its moon traced along

                        its hoof year after year

where words are beetles

                        and veins of air where

starry catfish come to breathe

                        coyote kept from lake weed

on the lip of its water

                        a freckle of time and jet stone

a glimmering tide

                        and a glimmering tide

PART TEN   SLAKE

a dead horse in sweet soil
cement mill

      if slake

a gun barrel knelt before
a thousand heat domes

      the thirst frankly,
      thirsts

PART ELEVEN   DECLARATION

I am   saguaro tall

cliff jade

moth wind

I listen to   ponds

cornfields

lynx mist

I come from   leaves rustling

clouded moons dissolving into nutsedge

I am   a stream of penstemon

salt flats

the song of water over rock

all gallows, only salt no pond or fog

no river

only sound

PART TWELVE   (BE)

I hold bleached clay to my lips
and mine the wash for more
I take to silt to the pews made of mud
my coal waste my tree rot

this, then a better warp
my hand against the tension
a silence between lightning and thunder

a dammed river there a dammed lung
a bridge a chemical a church
a slug a bullet a dynamite stick of the eye
a torso between my hands again

I turn from the loom
now a cellar spider
bent over antelope horn
and arrow grass

somewhere a voice calls
to say the ground cover is gone

hoots'aa', there is a depression (in a surface, as the ground).

hootso, pasture, meadow, pasturage.

hoozhónee, beauty way (ceremony).

hoozhooh, hozho, nahoozhooh, hoozhood, hodoozhooł,
hozhoooh, to become (be) peaceful, to become (be) harmonious.

HOOTSO

IF EMERGENCE

we look to the heavens
        from the north an arctic of geese

what we are told of time : thunder belongs to a spring storm
but in the swan range trumpets of cold wind
carry with it a winter call

this is the story we tell when seasons change
but what we are told of time : time is an ulcer
a lie we tell through mouths not our own
because this mouth belongs to policy
because time is stolen from us

someone said the morning is our one sole government
and still skies cling to thorn to utility pole
to my collarbone
to the promise of dawn

IF DESERT

and then the weather turned
red-bellied and plastic like my arms
with the amble of a drone beetle
night speak hellhound all done in and sour
a cold front spreads like mold
quick and in secret and just before its lip
a veil of sandbush and horseflies make a run for it
dust storms lope at the sprig
and spur of low hills
my reach bent mumbling something silver
future speak, marsh croak
even the moon is a bird of white shell
then blue stone flying through the haze of another wildfire
the world ending all along

IF HORSES NAMED WEATHER

Slipped through the lowland of a silvered night
I begged to keep just a piece of him
Begged to the shallow to the memory of soils
Houses turned over into mines beneath a highway
This is us when stretched across moss
Two rivers two rivers two rivers kissed

We are the pump and steam sometimes
I carry north horses named weather
Beg to ground doves to the chorus frogs we hear
The mountain bearings are never enough though
This baptism is what the church came for
A snowsquall the cottonwoods minnow-white

IF A FEELING, THEN A BELL DOME-SHAPED

Outside the city I limb and yaw the ellipses
of another drunken night

                              all reed and row and scurry

Outside the city, I climb and seal shut the paper-thin anxiety of
being alone with other men at a time like this : at least I was held

If a feeling, then a bell dome-shaped

If a feeling, then a corral of white horses
                deer deep in the sleep of my chest

IF CRANE

a gold moon beneath the black water laps at the surface
white cranes carry on their backs hope for another storm
dim clouds as tall as tomorrow sit mean over sand dunes
collapse on collapse – somewhere, the faint rain colors
another wildfire burning through the last juniper trees

it will be summer in no time

somewhere in a cornfield

I am bent like a waterbird

studying the way the moon

can be mistaken for a hole in the sky

IF FIRE

river brush floats on a big river in very little water
to the north a sleeper fire holdover from last season's wilds
bust sprout
       flame crawl
            the moon mistaken
                  for a hole in the sky :
                      if next world
                      still deer soften
                      into field field field
                      meadow hawk
                      rodent nests
                      overgrown undergrowth
                              all tinder is white space
                              its span a mirror
                              your mouth around light

IF THE END OF THE WORLD

through an open window
smoke settling in the leaves
like a bell ringing

IF HOPE WHAT THEN OF ITS BODY

in a field of wild grasses with colors only known in memory
we watch children grow up with salt held in their hands
they show us first that mud is baptismal mud can be new skin

but mud swallows even the most sacred sometimes

if hope what then of its body

      horse grass

                    lake waves

          evening light

                            hummingbirds

a barn door the new moon pressed shut

IF SENSES

look

see the sun
              scraped wallpaper
        green wind
                  damp soap on a shower wall

                                see hushed sage
                    needle bush
                                red brome

see silo

                      grain lost to echo
            see bike chains
                          wheelbarrows

        styrofoam melted in ash pits
            a glass of cold beer
                    a gold doorknob in morning light

see scour

                            train tracks
           tractor dust
                  see propane bottles

      redtop
        patches of rain
dyed wool

touch

the spooned
crow
swimming
in the pond
with sunfish
their spines
touching
the bottom
of the sky
at my feet
a mountain
licked
smooth
by
the monsoon
above it
the
memory
there
in the
rift-sawn
sand
shored
on its wing

taste

a splinter a bullet a dark hole
        lick clean
igneous rock water runoff an oil spill

a gender a wild rice a book
        tongue
copper mines chemtrail a squall line

a pedal an envelope a growing storm
        suck dry
the air a hurricane the sea

smell

horses   digging for water

horses   sinking into trees

horses   naming more horses

                                              singing

field   sinking into a name

field   digging for trees

field   naming water

                                    singing

morning digging

morning water sinking

morning naming all the trees

singing

listen

the door the winter oil the lung
the deer ; its leap its croon its thrush
its cold front an open porch

the clasp the entryway the collared sleeprock
the caress of another morning : its crash
its curtains dragged along a canyon wall

the splendor the yucca string the monument
the horses ; their lilt its halt their sigh
its low hum the trees all one labored breath

the aquarium the bottle of soda with peanuts
the hospital ; its gray overcast sky
the crying—oh, yes   the crying

then, dream

a beautiful land, free free free free

dream time unspooled from its barbed wire
      its border wall
               its pipeline
      its blockade

dream a thousand suns
>   even more their absence
>   dream the darkness
>>   how it carries the sound of us
>>   to the water

IF COLLAPSE

an arid moon beneath low water hung at the shore
cranes carry on their backs collapsed storm after storm
thin clouds fracked of tomorrow at the mercy of sand
collapse on collapse on lapse—the absence of rain colors
another wildfire burning through the memory of juniper

it will be winter in no time

somewhere in a dune field

I am hunched over like a comma

studying the way a landfill

can be mistaken for a sky

IF FIELD

in tender meadow light—stratum harked—now the ellipses yaw the wind's name / under a symphony of heatwaves dome-open / sunbeams shuck sound in glistening water / in the groove of it birds hush in endless field / day draped in the weeds like a painted morning

a liberation / a possibility / held in the hand like another hand

wasps formed elsewhere from bird or water lands
            where pine primordial, where topsoil cribbed
mud-black morning—its first skies more blue bark—
    an everlasting body against the brush, from it appeared
the first beetles and a grazing mist burned against cedar water
      the blush a lesser yellow—all stick and shell and abalone
or dry-sung corn seed, then another shell appeared
                and then another another another

ENTANGLEMENTS I

BEAR OIL DEER YUCCA

I

the code for man includes match or mirror
axe and needle

>he mines barrel
>he mines ore
>arsenic in my pelvis
>fracks shale rock beneath my ribs

he is a nosebleed in dirty snow
sun-grazed tar sands ant-lined deer bone or chokecherry

>his body a hay shed
>or sky stoned in firestorm
>kneeling into a valley garden
>of cattle and cordgrass

or a tree's hollow ached with worms no bullets
hunger, no song

II

apple
pretty
elk
ram
tooth
uncle
rabbit
eye

III

he asks to condemn time
before its gospel compels grasses to ash to dust

coal rock breathing
beneath wandering myths and microbursts
rivers, the rivers stealing sediment
from words at the wrist

he demands I blink open the cloud in every letter
and again they turn into his lips on mine

inside him a language
moans open
ripgut and copper
zipped into a key

this is not the first time you will kneel
before a man like him this is not the first
time you will kneel before a man like him
this is not the first time you will kneel before a man like him

IV

his head in closet light and apartment parking lots
morning after morning

each one
he meets at night
to deliver a prayer
he cannot tongue

he feels the reach of it in the middle of a hailstorm
columns of cloud howling in the east

he leaks onto the bedsheet
in slow river

                        yellow metal
                   in the current

SAND DUNE MIGRATION RATES AND THE DOOR TO MY BEDROOM AS A CHILD

on the bevel on a broken stone

one torn gray overcast sky in the hospital tile

floodwaters on the roadway

somewhere elk ate up the monsoons

and left behind soap smell and some rabbits culling

I stand alone in a broken field

the taste of him and smog in my mouth

the myriad of ways I pray for parentheses

someone to parent all of this

someone to stop the sand hilled on the snow

GHOST LAKE

periphery, there—a long garden
it's cliché to say we bloom
for each other {   } when I do more
of the blooming

my throat caved
under the puff of skull I call a skull
inside, the cranium carries cerebrum
logic reasoning as in I should've left you

{

}

there {   } a long garden, lush
locked, an oasis of an oasis there
and we {   } our torsos
touching in the tickseed

never touching though
a wildfire burns along the highway
in our memory of each other
you come closer to the asphalt

you say—
there is smoke in my body
still you say I can feel it
the smoke in my body

I mistake the smoke for winter fog
this is what you wanted right
you wanted to be my breath
and we {   } to sate our hunger

{

            }

there was a lake here you say
I repeat there was a lake here
as if to at least see my voice touch yours
and you trace my lip with your {   }

there {   } a lake here
and just because there isn't anymore
doesn't mean we don't feel
the water echo beneath us

A MOTH-COLORED HORSE

We started in form : his lips tremble on my collar pocket
        in the back seat of winter light

On our way to the lake, a moth horse on the roadway
        broken bloom for eyes
        it carried night shawled on its back

At the lake, I mention to him the morning
        chamisa bushes in my voice

I horse a floodway through him before we drive along
        early light back to the homes we forgot
        and the cities we left behind

I remember the sound of his teeth.

That the sky had tasted of me.

He told me the moth horse was the sound of my name :

Gravel smoke nested in my body behind a cold window.

AFTER DARK

he crosses night –
field of wild antennae
fireweed shadscale

the dirt beneath has teeth
root and stem
television static

he calls to me
with the sounds
of wet alligator juniper

he calls my name
with the beak break of a crow
cocking its head to the south

long leadplant
and saltbush
he tells me my name

his name is mercury
his head sky-thick
not yet cloud nor rain

his skull is a shelf
for white candles
an unlocked gun box

half-full fifth of dark matter
a late evening gnat sung
sweet dark soil and wolftail

desert prickly pear
a bloated dust storm
his name after dark

his build a mountain peak
over meadow sleepgrass
narrow shoot and switchback

he carries into his core
belt burn nectarines
and even moro smoke

I learn to love him
so erosive it eats
through the canyon

like pink water
níłtsą bi'áád
slow over peach rock

the field stands taller
when he turns key to engine
and tells me he dances

too many sorrows
through open windows
where jackrabbits ash

at the hem sown
with thin ragweed
and a sunken backroad

he drives off
mottles the horizon
as if chancel

as if sunrise
as if all of it
 – all its beauty

A WALK IN TSAILE

the sun fails to make sense anymore

                          an insect buzzes in overgrown red brome

butterfly whistle   beetle spark or wire rush

                     cattle choke on wild sage far in late weather

wide meadow and big sky

                             little water wrong with words

and wind and a faded scar

                   like the one I trace on your wrist sometimes

and man the day fell hours ago

                              and you ask me to slow down

something shifts in the bushes

                     a rabbit   an eternity   a bull snake

there is a meteorite in my hand

                                   a sparrow in yours

EMERGING

Act I: Níyol

Dah 'adíí'ą́ągo dá'ák'ehgóó deeshwoł.

Act II: Chahałheeł

Once upon a time, { five-fingered being   cold air   sunrise } stepped into a sentence: Nizhónígo bi'éé' holǫ́ǫ dooleeł. Éé'tsoh diłhiłgo yii'doohnah. They stepped further into the words. There is water; łeets'aa' nímazí shee hólǫ́. There is a meadow, a winter's meadow, gathering in a bright morning.

Act III: Dą́ą́n

Shándíín;
Hootsoh bits'ą́'dinídíín.
Saad 'adííłhéelgo yiiłtsą́.

Act IV: Shí

Bóhoosh'aah
I stand in the sun
with an empty bowl
meant for a river

HE SAID MY NAME

He said my name is really a kiln, a haul of groundwater
because mouths open into hot vapor. He said my name
is actually a riverbed. He said to make of my name a choking
of cracked ice. He said to say my name is old water in a ditch.

He said to make of my name a peach tree on fire, a palm
of pollen. He said my name is really an aquifer, an aster field,
an orchestra of damp tarps in a sheep corral, a downed pole
in Rocksprings. He said my name is as tall as a smokestack.

He said my name tends to cause a draft, to be a touch of tequila.
He said my name is reed, heavy blue mornings
in June. He said to make of my name wildfire smoke.
He said my name is rumor, the low beams of a pickup.

He said my name is really a sermon of locusts, boulder rust
in a river gorge. He said to make of my name a desert garden.
He said my name is the one pink evening when you whisper
your name to the moon and it whispers back in monsoon.

SOFT THUNDER

Narrow-mouth toads dapple pink sandstone
Knee-deep in a brown bowl of brown water

Before the croon of limb and wind on weeds
Puddles from the pour gather for a morning song

The sun rises from a flatbed load of open palms
    :   each crease a ripple a leg a half smile

The sun knows best when it rises
    :   each tide and oak and uplift sung the same

Each killdeer and mare and desert bighorn
Each I I gorge each I I ravine each I I—

            and each part of me is hung out to dry
              marooned and wrung of rain

        wrung of every I until no I is left
           soft thunder ponds in a clearing

THE RATE AT WHICH LAND IS LOST TO DROUGHT LIKE A HAND ACROSS HIS LIPS

there is microplastic in my name
there is a drought in his
long like the letter *b* unbound

a tension keeps along the dull blade of an echo
enough to stall a supercell
the shadow of a storm
caught in the valley of its premise:

    we see it along the interstate
        a dark body the color of gunmetal
another blue otherworldly and clean
        of its mourning

there is memorial in his veins
along the back of his knee
a bull snake stretches long into the daytime
to coil the air as if an engine

    at the end of the day
    at the end of our wake
    I pull thread from the shore of his puff and panting
        I lick clean an oil funnel

FROM AUTUMN

I wonder the language of light on a late-morning walk in what
feels like the desert willow of winter;
ash – flow – bellow tuff – velvet mesquite : The mountain in
the distance the color of the world. Wind is the language of sky,
heard through sentences, through tumbleweeds :
What is water if not the sky looking at itself?

                     A warbler sees itself in me, in my throat, or am
I just the trick of light; ran rampant through a whisper of river?
Something made alive by voice? : But what is voice if not wind?
a low lake – collide – joy – wit – wing – joy – only morning
And now let me explain in Navajo : The moon is a penny. I
carry with me an empty notebook meant for the coming clouds;
the pages held between the breaths of the silver I feel choked and
collapsed when I walk on damp wood chips and frozen mud. I
walk between two houses in favor of the other; and by the time I
reach one

it's near noon

and there's a rabbit cloaked in sawdust
murmuring through a snowy field

not a bird in the sky

Only the face of memory:
All the colors of every single morning

OPENING LIGHT

gravity is god deep-felt but impossible to see
what might be true what joy :
    two birds rigged to cloud
    lake shimmer wind kept in dust fog

there are monsters sometimes still deep inside people
              opening light thundering through

say this is a step into silence
toward beauty and *beauty* and everlasting
    the air the color of canyon peach
    a rain-lit morning in open field

In the beginning, breath – erosive slather of wind and vein.
                      Waters saint the church caught at the throat,
callus, calcium, a bitter tide. The first body bent
    into locust into tower : a mountain physics, an early river.

A mother with a humming pulse, uranium holy, conjures
                  the first atom. Then pelvis, backbone, smoke,
a leg's language. The letters stand and stretch
        at first thunder, womb geometry : even more water

Time gusts through the pulpit at a woven voice box.
    Its old alphabet steps into a warbling current and listens
to the first word flung from an open hand.
                Its mouth pedals open around the sound,
one single cicada click above the water :   *tó*

AND STILL DEER SOFTEN

SEARCHING FOR TRUTH IN THE MORNING

                        in the east
a cornfield wrinkles a quiet snow
passing ice and hail silk cattle white
beyond the sunflower thread fence
                              a hilltop of morning
dews the burst line of piñon and big sage

in the cloud place a sky just opened in low blue
                                          never just blue
drawn out by cicada and brome harp and hummingbird
the only truth around here is dark moss damp warm
beneath squash bugs holding light on their backs

WHERE DO WILD HORSES LIVE

Not near canyons or slaughterhouses
Not at the salt lick
    Interstate highways
Not deer
Not elk
Not erosion or overgrazing
Not wild elsewhere
      Sheep in the valley
          Nor any waters

ANTHROPOCENE: A DICTIONARY

Dibé bighan: sheep corral

juniper beams caught charcoal in the late-summer morning
night still pooled in hoofprints; deer panicked run from water

Ooljéé' bist'ą'dinídíín: moonlight

perched above the town drowned in orange and streetlamp
the road back home dips with the earth
shines black in the sirens

Bit'a' : its sails or—its wing (s)

        driving through the mountain pass
                dólii, mountain bluebird, swings out—
     from swollen branches

I never see those anymore, someone says

Diyóół   : wind (

wind (more of it) more wind as in (to come up)
plastic bags driftwood the fence line

Nihootsoii

        :   evening—somewhere northward fire
                        twists around the shrublands;
                sky dipped in smoke—twilight

there is a word for this, someone says

: Deidíílid   they burned it

: Ákódeiilyaa   we did this

ON RAIN OR LIGHT OR JOY

Yes, I made it rain. At the horizon a broom or brume of light
this is the rain, for which we kneeled to someone who came back
from the dead[1] so yes I made it rain (I am here, alive) so yes the
rain comes through me and only me, every night in fact / The
rain is a story of survival

so once it stops so do I and so do you
but for now, take my hand lapping at the evening[2]
the light is raining

through accordion light the shadows of ghosts of ghosts
through accordion light an altar of or alter to windmill mornings
through accordion light the absence of it
through accordion light a sentence sentence-ing

This is my face.

A liquor of light, a lacquer of it.
This is my face, an entire song of it

> Go my son, go and climb the ladder.
> Go my son, go and earn your feather.
> Go my son, make your people proud of you. [3]

This is my body: loam, pond-quiet, text contorted into a crane on water, a sinew of light attached to another and to another to beyond and has been and ever after / but for now, the wind crumbles into drought and evenings last longer, sometimes all night[4]—a town breathing, cactus hum, panicgrass afoot (dancing, dancing, dying, dancing some more)

For now, go out and dream of joy, we know the labor of feeling it

1   see present joy present joy present joys, a murmur of it, enough to fill a stadium
2   take its hand, let go of mine
3   a different name for mourning, a different name for joy
4   tsídii ga'ayáásh dootł'ízhii
      kogaa' ashiłní
      nídiidááh shitsoí
      hayíílką́ shiłní

KÉYAH : SAAD

In this essay, I will

—locate the land's locution
—shimmer inside a word's mineral
—make my home sentence twine
—turn possessives into antiquated vocabulary

In this essay, I will

leave this place—

the desert is no sea its glimmer only black rock
knelt at the skycase
a chimney of sun tar and asphalt
beneath the rake and roll of cactus and canyon seed
spring dew taunts tarantula and scorpion
parched in a midday temperature high
for springtime or late fall

In this essay,

the desert is a love letter
there is no sea
a desert undertow is thirst
its riptide a dust devil
the light casts its name in tarmac
swarm and memory

In this something other than *essay*

somewhere there is a fire
about to happen or is happening or has happened

In this   *I will*

this is the high desert, i.e., a place with light
so much of it we forgot how to look

In this desert, I will

light the hardened meadow with a technology so ancient we call
it language.

This is what I mean:
the field steps pink onto a hairline road
the sun washed on morning needle and wrestled sap
it was an early frost followed by late heat
there are no rules or boundaries out here

the trees at the tree line are only a border
if we say it is – the same goes for river or alcove

If the lights go off any one moment, would we fear
the darkness? In it, we can't see the cornfields
empty of corn or weeds growing in the abandoned mine.

In this darkness, I will

write a love letter to winter and call it by its real name
language, after all, is the only sound it can hear

I will say I am from here, this desert, a home
I refuse to let a border town be my name

Where are you from, they'll ask
Háádę́ę́'shą' naniná?

Here, I'll say. *Everywhere –*

COMING ACROSS A HORNED TOAD

when I saw a horned toad
watch wildfire on juniper corpse
its eyes mattered pitched
and smoldered open

its name echoed small blood
a room full of breathing
a fire-caught voice
the body is a river is a body

horizon shrouded suddenly
tongue carried into mountain
into memory veined dusk bone spur
a moon trail touch-lit

another cathedral
another paint coat cracking
another
another

I have a tin can for sky
settled in open prisms
prisms between storm
and a god

I still see clouds still
over valley dirt afternoons
in December
when evening turns a dark shore

everything tall
through the piñons
I take note
because it comes back

comes lunar becomes
ash altered in spilled morning
because bloom
because white trees

because rope soot
a river's winded teeth
placid silver
and ankle-deep

under baptized skies
of black dirt
I hear morning
shell blue

and there a horned toad
its skin its flat time
its spine its arrowhead
pollen on its back

or is it sleet rain
braiding along
a dense prayer
I carry morning

AMERICA

my mom & aunts sing along to Waylon Jennings, making tortillas in the kitchen. They say they never really went to school because boarding school never counts. They say drain the sink water, demand I open a window. They say they don't know how to dance, asking how to pronounce 'oppressed.'
The dough hangs from their hands crusted with flour,

        starlight,   cracked bushes,   yucca bloom,
                       mudstone,   fox sparrows,
night storms drowned out by frogs in song

                                      thew

        hum

                      bellow

        molt   hush

                    coo

DAYBREAK

K'ad abíní hoolzhish

: the low-moon horizon turquoise serenes pink-lit from the pulp and fray of whorled milkweed summer cypress turkey-feathered struts stark pebbled through the sheep corral and shade house beneath the horse trough star thistle and nine-awned grass reflect night storms and rainbow through the morning, sunrays darling through narrow shoots of cloud, vapor, or maybe morning fog

Hók'ą́ą́dóó

: above a passing plane or marsh hawk or maybe a crow casts its wing on the sweet yellow clover and field weed, under the rubble of rust tin can and car axle and wheelbarrow a downed basketball backboard crafted from sheet metal and piping the ground crickets and moths tell a story as butterflies they flail and flare through two-needle piñon and ryegrass cottontails squirrel into the culvert under the main road parched wash-like its flow sands really memory for water

K'ad i'íí'ą́

: salsify and velvetweed overtop a broken fence its twine slat and barbed wire cloaked by dusked sod dirt road mud walls or tumbleweed and maybe sunflowers bow-pulled arc by the metal windmill watering faint wind the mill echoes awake with each rock thrown at its face or back or the bend of its opened arms – bįįh níléíjí da'ayą́ – clouds drop their shoulders into rain into the coral evening, into the evening's evening

AGAIN APOCALYPSE

One

rain leaves a woven rug made of sand at the bottom of the wash

the storms sit down in a floodplain of sediment shoot
        a name of caliche and saline alluvial soils

the storm's face, the hardpan leached of its memories
        its sumac its peaches

you sit down to call someone inside your house a few yards east
        but the person you call is made of humus too

be wild you think to yourself before you feel bluestem
        trace the lining of your foot

lightning though the lightning overflows from any canyon
        any low-lying wash

you step into the open field
        feel the sun flat on the land

how does this look on fire?
        you promise we can put it out.

how can we? our hands are stitched to the memory of water
        move and it might tick

Two

in a region of mild winters plants die
        or rather the heat sink of it all drains the roots
        of their breathing

in a region of mild winters people find trees
        that are never just trees
        an anchor to this world
        a pathway to the next

in a region of mild winters no more bears but moose
        on the ridgeline
        bomb cyclones on their backs

in a region of mild winters infinity caught in the bottomlands
        its ornate cape foliated with only memories
        that's called a downburst someone says frantically

Three

The past well-deep and open-eyed mends the mill of memory

The morning's mouth drawn with the map of deep bone

A mouth along the raw makeup of compost: eggshell or egg salad

In the layer of concrete thousands of years from now: what science
        belonged here   what view of a city on fire

Perhaps across winter sand someone will make of this cough
        a diagram an installation without any walls

        its maze an open room in which one might surmise
        a century holding its own breath
                as if in shock
                as if someone had died
                as if another bomb dropped
                the glass shattering all around

And maybe in some window to this life you see yourself
        summon a small smile
                maybe a crane looped above a pond
                Oh, look, a bee –
                Actually, that's soot,
                the bees have gone

Four

it's a topographic map you think
        the hilltops make out the neural waves of the space
                around you –
        the landscape is not just a landscape

        it's the person you meant to call but they didn't answer
        during the latest wave of monsoon storms

        and still they sit waiting dressed up in flash floods
        or mudslides, the purple of the fabric stained like blood

this time, though, you feel the water and its spines on your neck
        even though you've been inside the whole time

welcome to the apocalypse you laugh to yourself
        upstream a wall of sorrow is unleashed
        a doing of the sky

ANTHROPOCENIC

: when the nearest light is miles away yet
    and adorned on the night is a lightning bug
        as in jarred cactus plants
      an open book without commas

: when the only thing you can touch is a plastic raft
    and drenched between the hours is a cutting board
        as in a place for garlic
      and onions the face of early sky

: when waters break into tar sands
    and to one long tune acacia trees dance some
        as in alder and its reach
      anything is worth the rain

: when above more and more narrow miracles
    and answers set to stone by a single hand
        as in a chorus of them
      any shadow still means light

SURFACE MAPPING

In the beginning, breath—wind, more wind, as if breath—
a doing of sky, its name on the wind but it doesn't rain anymore.

I remember snow chest-high on the horses, their bodies marooned
and dark across the white space—letters splashed on the face of a
forgotten sky; piñon shells singing on a plastic tarp; the darker
marks across my back.

There is no water, I can't breathe through the smoke haze the fog a
burden of time layered like the tree rings on my fingertip

This is how they will remember us : water barrels and basins;
coal burning in the lungs; dust pneumonia, a shifting sand dune;
a dune field dry streambeds sand on little snow evaporation rates,
silt at the bottom of muscle spasms; where words are beetles :

    I happen across
a dead crow a dead horse
        and still deer soften

FIELD SONG

I carry the. When we get to the water, then. I open—a field
leaps through the cunning ebbs of collapse. I carry light.
A boy born of drought, when we get to the water, the water

    light like moths across our shoulders, like morning,
this time however a wildfire is burning at sunset. This time,
I crawl into the smoke. This time, I carry all the careful wind.

When we get to the dead horses, I suppose the wind
is felt, deep blue within the silt of it—when we get to the field,
I close any shutter left open. Though, this time

    I spin the silk of water beetles into the kind of light
we see on the rangelands, where morning unravels into morning.
When we get to the. When we get. When we get to the water,

I kneel before the century of us, every molecule begins to water
and, before us, a bridge opens to another world. A new wind—
not carried in dust storms—this wind walks in like the morning

      where we find it. I carry. I open the. Into the sullen field
I ask you to follow me as though I know a way through. Light
like frog songs on the warped crescendo of leaves, this time

falling through the sky like birds, each one a sound. This time
when we get to the. I look to blue horses. The water
only a memory for now. I ask for a glass at the counter. The light

      in the diner the color of the doom we feel : but in the wind
there is hope, like a moon opening her eye, ants washed in field
song. When we get to. It's morning on top of another morning.

I carry. What really is left after all of this dries up is the morning
and a mirror—a dimension we catch day after day, time after time :
and in the *after*time, I hope to watch you walk in this very field
    where words are beetles and still deer soften. The water,
when we get to it, is flooding the wash after a heavy storm. Wind
just enough to spur along more song in a beautiful afternoon light.

When we get to the water of the next world, the sunset light
will be pink just like how we remember it. Every single morning
birds will leap out of the cupboards. Soon, a stronger wind
    will bring along the storms, their dresses heavy with time.
I suppose the brim will be that of pollen when we get to the water.
The sky pronounced on red soil. I open my mouth. I open the field.

I am nothing but wind. My voice carried in its light.

A door crickets and sprawls in an open field. I carry morning.

We happen across a bluebird this time when we get to the water.

NOTES

Contexts

In 2018, approximately 191 horses were found dead at a stock pond on the Navajo Nation. The horses were identified as feral horses, wild horses, or free-roaming horses. Stock ponds are used as water stations for roaming livestock in what has been called an arid landscape. The stock pond where the horses were found was near Gray Mountain in Northern Arizona. It had been dry because of the extreme drought the Navajo Nation is facing, caused by decades-long aggression by the United States and the changing climate. The horses were found thigh- and neck-deep in the mud, some horses on top of other horses.

> *These animals were searching for water to stay alive. In the process,theyunfortunatelyburrowedthemselvesintothemud and couldn't escape because they were so weak.*
> – Former Navajo Nation President Jonathan Nez

The horses were found in a circle, mud caked in their coats. Some horses were found upright as if running. The Navajo Nation, as a response, sprayed the horses with hydrated lime to speed up decomposition and buried the horses on-site. Today, the feral horse problem is contributing to the drought conditions of the Navajo Nation.

One horse survived and her name is Grace.

The horses, in a circle, gathering gathering gathering.

Sand dune migration in the Navajo Nation is a contributing factor to the drought conditions on the reservation. Since the early 2000s, sand dunes have grown by seventy percent and continue to kill off remaining rare and endangered plant life, overtake entire roads and homes, and destabilize any farm or pastures on the reservation.

The cornfield where I grew up is nothing but sand. When I was researching the feral horse problem, I came across a Facebook thread where folks were debating what to do to about the horses. In a response to the idea that horses should be treated as sacred animals and be left alone, one person commented, 'There is nothing but sand here.' Overgrazing is a significant issue and grouped with the extreme drought and shifting sand dunes, plant life is dwindling at a rapid pace. Soon, there might be nothing but sand as more and more rivers and streams leave behind beds of fine sand. As the winds kick up because of changing climate, more and more sand will shroud the reservation and surrounding areas, resulting in poorer air quality and dust pneumonia.

In one NGS study, Navajo elders discussed how the monsoon storms and winter snowstorms were more cyclical. They talked about the abundance of rain and snow that came with the wind. This, when traced back to the beginning of time, is connected to the belief that sacred winds are given to us at birth and these winds give us our voice, our language.

And now, what now? Wind and sand. More wind.

Composition

The book is composed using specific numbers that are important in Diné thought and lifeway: numbers two, four, six, twelve. The triptych is also used to purposely warp and disrupt the design of the book. These numbers make up the structure of the book. For example, some poems have four sections and the opening poem,

'Horses,' is a twelve-part poem. Other forms were used in the book, and each is related, in some way, to these numbers.

Translations for various Diné words and phrases were sourced from Quanah Yazzie and various Navajo dictionaries. I relied on simple sentences in this volume as I'm not a fluent speaker of Diné and I want to be clear as to not posit that I am somehow a scholar, in any sense of the word, of Diné worldview or linguistic structure. I, in fact, know nothing. I am learning though and these poems helped me. For more, see 'A Failed Glossary.'

Punctuation and its absence are used with purpose, like all white space.

A FAILED GLOSSARY

The only true glossary you need for this book is your ear or your eye. Perhaps, the small grooves ink makes on paper that you can feel when you trace your finger along the word's shape.

The act of translation is slippery. I think of it as *refraction,* to borrow from Jennifer S. Cheng. For example, your body is a translation of every hand placed upon it. However, I do believe that some poems could be taught because of their use of Diné Bizaad (Navajo Language).

Translations (in the order they appear):

Níyol : Wind

Dah 'adíí'ą́ą́go dá'ák'ehgóó deeshwoł : I will walk into a field at noon

Chahałheeł : Darkness

Nizhónígo bi'éé' holǫ́ǫ dooleeł : They will have beautiful clothes

Éé'tsoh diłhiłgo yii'doohnah : They put on a dark jacket

Łeets'aa' nímazí shee hóló : I have a bowl

Dą́ą́n : Spring

Shándíín : Sunlight

Hootsoh bits'ą́'dinídíín : Light shining from a meadow

Saad 'adíílhéelgo yiiłtsą : I see a row of words

Shį́ : Summer

Bóhoosh'aah : I am learning

K'ad abíní hoolzhish : It's morning now

Hók'ą́ą́dóó : From above

K'ad i'íí'ą́ : It's evening

Bįįh níléíjí da'ayą́ : Deer are eating over there

ON THE POEMS

The line 'just before the silence' is borrowed from the album title *Just Before Silence* by Suso Saiz & Menhir.

'Horses' is a twelve-part poem that is comprised of various works inspired by other poets. Part Four, I can attribute to Layli Long Soldier. Part Seven is inspired by Michael McGriff's 'Why I Am Obsessed with Horses'. Most of the book was comprised using McGriff's 'Image List' exercise. Part Eleven is the result of a writing exercise designed by Kinsale Drake.

The text on page 19 comes from *The Navajo Language: A Grammar and Colloquial Dictionary* by Robert W. Young and William Morgan.

'In the beginning' is inspired by the opening poem to Sherwin Bitsui's *Flood Song*.

'Hootso' is a section comprised of twelve separate poems. In 'If Senses', the sixth sense is dreaming, which is considered a sense in Diné worldview per Diné scholar Carlos Teller.

'Bear Oil Deer Yucca' was composed using code words developed by the Navajo Code Talkers in WWII.

'A Walk in Tsaile' is after C. D. Wright as is most of the book.

The poem 'Wasps formed elsewhere' on page 49 is comprised of words taken from various English translations (often exploitative and done by non-Diné anthropologists) of the Diné creation stories. It's a reclamation.

'On Rain or Light or Joy' is a poem in response to Sky Hopinka's work *I'll Remember You as You Were, not as What You'll Become* and includes lines borrowed from the film and lines borrowed from the poem 'Sure You Can Ask Me a Personal Question' by the poet Diane Burns. The manuscript version includes lyrics from the song 'Go My Son' written and performed by Arlene Nofchissey Williams and Carnes Burson.

'Where Do Wild Horses Live' is a poem comprised of found language from comments posted to a public Facebook thread about feral horses on the Navajo Nation.

'Field Song' is a sestina with the words 'field', 'light', 'water', 'morning', 'time', and 'wind' as the repeated end words. These words make up the words that are used the most throughout the collection.

ACKNOWLEDGEMENTS

I thank the various journals and magazines that published versions of these poems. I also want to thank the John and Renée Grisham Writers in Residence program for supporting my completion of this book. Thanks to Mary Austin Speaker and Canisia Lubrin for helping me shape this book.

This book wouldn't be possible without poets who have inspired me. I would not be a poet without the works and writings of so many Diné poets and writers. It would take a lifetime talking about these artists and their impact. I plan to do just that.

I specifically want to acknowledge the books *Blue Horses Rush In* by Luci Tapahonso, *Blue Horses for Navajo Women* by Nia Francisco, and *She Had Some Horses* by Joy Harjo that oriented my writing of this book toward hope and everlasting morning. The title was also inspired by the album *Horses* by Patti Smith.

This book is dedicated to my family and friends. You know who you are.

I wanted this book to be about the end of the world and I realized it might be about a new one, caught somewhere at the horizon, like the morning, all blue and crisp. It's calling to us; if we listen hard enough, we will hear it.

akoya

An Independent Publishing House

Akoya celebrates courageous, visionary
and innovative writing from
around the world.

We are a home for authors and
translators, not just their books.

Discover more from Akoya at

www.akoyapublishing.com

Akoya Publishing
222 Kensal Road
London
W10 5BN

Copyright © Jake Skeets, 2026
First published in the United States of America as *Horses*
by Milkweed Editions in 2026
First published in the UK
by Akoya Publishing Ltd in 2026

The right of Jake Skeets to be identified as the author
of this work has been asserted by him in accordance
with Section 77 of the Copyright, Designs and
Patents Act 1988

Paperback ISBN 978-1-83675-010-9
Ebook ISBN 978-1-83675-022-2

Design by Holly Titchener
Text design by Phil Cleaver
Typeset in 10.08/14.4pt Egizio URW
by Six Red Marbles UK, Thetford, Norfolk
Printed and bound in Lithuania
by Balto print

1 3 5 7 9 10 8 6 4 2

All rights reserved. No part of this publication may
be reproduced, stored or transmitted in any form
or by any means without prior written permission
from the publisher.

A CIP record for this book is available
from the British Library.

The authorised representative in the EEA is eucomply
OÜ Pärnu mnt 139b-14 11317 Tallinn, Estonia.
hello@eucompliancepartner.com
+337 576 90241

akoyapublishing.com